impressions

FARCOUNTRY

photography by **Steven Kazlowski**

D0624512

Dedication

I dedicate this book to my mother for teaching me to keep going with a smile and a tear.
                    Steven Kazlowski

The terms "brown bear" and "grizzly bear" refer to the same species of animal. The former term applies to coastal bears, while the latter are inland bears.

RIGHT: A sea otter cradles her pup in Prince William Sound. Sea otters frequently groom, rest, and nurse young while floating on their backs.

TITLE PAGE: A bull moose surveys its territory in Denali National Park. The moose was made the official Alaska land mammal in 1998.

FRONT COVER: Polar bear cub playing with whale baleen. Polar bears dine primarily on seals, but they also feast on stranded whales and scavenge dead animals.

BACK COVER: Dall ram on the rocky slopes of Denali National Park. The winter diet for Dall sheep consists mostly of dry, frozen grass and sedge stems not covered by snow.

ISBN 1-56037-283-4
Photographs © 2004 Steven Kazlowski
© 2004 Farcountry Press

For more information on our books write
Farcountry Press, P.O. Box 5630, Helena, MT 59604,
call (800) 821-3874, or visit www.farcountrypress.com

Created, produced, and designed in the United States.
Printed in China.

Foreword

by Andrew J. Scott

Baby hare, or leveret.

*F*amilies of polar bears gather along the Alaskan coast, gnawing on washed-up whale bones. The cubs play chase, box, bump, and wrestle until one runs back to its mother, feeling outdone.

An arctic fox, its coat white as the snow, waits, sniffs, then leaps high into the air, pouncing on its prey.

Herds of caribou lumber across brightly colored wild flowers of the tundra, migrating for the season.

Alaska remains wild—too big and too harsh to tame. Derived from the native word "Alyeska," meaning "great land," Alaska is often called the Last Frontier, a place yet to be conquered. Gold prospectors, trappers, and oil interests all braved the harsh land in search of riches. But even into the twenty-first century, much of Alaska remains a wilderness.

This is still a mythical, lonely place—the land of the midnight sun. Distant snow-covered mountain ranges loom beyond miles of desolate tundra. Color flashes across winter night skies – the Northern Lights. Wolves howl in the darkness.

The terrain is vast, the climate harsh and varied. At 570,373 square miles, Alaska is more than twice the size of Texas. Home to the highest peak in North America—Mount McKinley (Denali)—the state boasts thirty-nine mountain ranges. Thawing tundra breeds great swarms of mosquitoes in the summer. Northern ice packs provide a winter habitat. Some dry interior lands are considered deserts, while hemlock and spruce blanket southeastern Alaska in a lush green rainforest. Along the coasts, glaciers flow and retreat over the ages. Over 3 million lakes dot the land.

Alaskan animals adapt to the land and to each other—a gigantic ecosystem displayed in subtle ways. On the coast, nutrient-rich waters attract fish. The fish become food for many: for the whales, splashing their great tails up through the surface as they dive; for thousands of bald eagles, soaring and swooping down to the water; and for barking sea lions along the shore. On the winter ice packs of the northern coast, an arctic fox follows a polar bear, waiting for scarce leftovers of a kill. Trailing behind, the tiny fox mimics the massive 1,200-pound bear, like a child following an older sibling.

The wonder of Alaska's wildlife is captured through the camera of Steven Kazlowski, a photographer who is at home in the most remote territory. Educated as a marine biologist but born with a sense of adventure, Steven finds Alaska's wildlife in its many beautiful settings—migratory birds in the Arctic National Wildlife Refuge, Dall sheep clinging to cliffs of the Brooks Range, red foxes, moose, and musk oxen on the interior tundra, marine life along the fjords of the Kenai Peninsula, sea otters on the bleak Aleutian Islands. These photos capture Steven's *Alaska Wildlife Impressions*.

Red fox kits.

The spread of the horns of this musk ox shows that it is a young bull. Musk oxen spend the entire winter in small, tight groups on the Alaskan Arctic Coast, where the temperatures may reach 70 below zero for weeks at a time.

ABOVE: King eiders on a tundra pond in the Central Arctic Coastal Plain in spring. Males sport black-and-white patterns; eider hens are brown to rust-colored, with black bars and mottling that aids concealment during nesting.

RIGHT: After feasting on a duck, the photographer observed that this peregrine falcon was too heavy to fly off a grassy island in the middle of an icy pond.

ABOVE: Bull caribou ready to shed its antlers. Large bulls lose their antlers in late October, while small bulls and non-pregnant cows do so in April.

RIGHT: Hoary marmots spend spring and summer on talus slopes, where the rocks provide cover from predators and also serve as look-out posts. This marmot near Exit Glacier has spotted the photographer.

ABOVE: A gray male wolf and a black female wolf put their traveling on pause; this pair covered ten miles in one hour. As elusive as they are beautiful, wolves in the wild are one of the most difficult animals to photograph.

LEFT: The Alaskan peninsula is one of the last strongholds of the brown bear. This sow in Katmai National Park prowls the incoming tide for salmon to feed to its hungry triplets.

FACING PAGE: A humpback whale breaches in the waters off Kenai Fjords National Park. Breaching is thought to be a form of communication between humpbacks.

BELOW: A juvenile bald eagle shares a perch with an adult. The conspicuous white head and tail are not attained until five or more years of age.

A pair of female musk oxen on the Central Arctic Coastal Plain huddle
together for security from grizzlies and wolves.

Under the midnight sun, this sandhill crane leads the photographer
away from its nest of newly hatched chicks.

ABOVE: A curious young red fox in the Central Alaskan Brooks Range. Red foxes can be distinguished from other species by the characteristic white-tipped tail, present regardless of color phase. Red is the most common coat color, but fur can vary from light yellowish to deep auburn red.

LEFT: Dall sheep graze while storm clouds approach in Denali National Park.

ABOVE: Newly hatched oyster catcher sits helpless on the beach in Kenai Fjords National Park—its camouflage of gray down is its only defense.

RIGHT: This rock ptarmigan blends perfectly with its wintery environment. In summer, its wings remain white but its body turns brown.

In spring, Brant geese travel to their nesting grounds in the north.

ABOVE: Two yearling polar bear cubs play in the golden light of morning in the Arctic National Wildlife Refuge.

LEFT: A sow polar bear and cub make their way across a frozen lagoon on the Coastal Plain of the Arctic National Wildlife Refuge. Polar bears are solitary most of the year, with the exception of females with their young.

ABOVE: A harbor seal rests on an ice flow that has calved from a glacier, Kenai Fjords National Park.

LEFT: When diving, humpback whales lift their flukes out of the water, creating a froth of seawater. While most humpbacks stay below the surface for no more than 15 minutes, some stay submerged for as long as 30 minutes.

FACING PAGE: Bald eagles gather along a sand spit on Kachemak Bay to search for Alaska resident Jean Keene, who lives on the sand spit and gives them their daily winter feeding of fish. More than 300 eagles gather just outside Homer to spend the winter with Keene.

BELOW: This whistling swan preens its feathers in the sunshine. Whistling swans nest on tundra mounds throughout the Arctic Coast.

A bull moose steps out of the cool of a pond in Denali National Park. Males in prime condition weigh between 1,200 and 1,600 pounds and are quite dangerous during rutting season.

RIGHT: A black bear roams the slopes above a glacier in Kenai Fjords National Park to feed on vegetation. Black bears, which can vary in color from blue-black to cinnamon, are most easily distinguished from brown bears by their straight facial profile and sharply curved claws, which are rarely longer than one and a half inches.

BELOW: A newly hatched clutch of pintail ducks awake from a nap in the Tetlin Wildlife Refuge.

ABOVE: A hoary marmot dines on lupine buds and flowers, both high in nutrients, in Kenai Fjords National Park.

FACING PAGE: This musk ox cow and newborn settle into the snow under the midnight sun on the Central Arctic Coastal Plain. Calves are born in early spring in temperatures below zero degrees.

This brown bear rests on the tidal flats at low tide in Katmai National Park. Brown bears rely heavily on salmon as a food source, and they scour the surrounding streams for the nutritious fish.

An arctic fox hunts on the Central Arctic Coastal Plain. The photographer watched this fox sniff and listen to the ground, then suddenly leap through the air and pounce on its prey.

Steller's sea lions on the Chiswell Islands. Males weigh an average
of 1,245 pounds, while females average 579 pounds.

A lesser Canada gosling practices swimming in the waters of
this marsh on the Central Arctic Coastal Plain.

Regal and proud, these two bald eagles on Kachemak Bay scan their surroundings for prey.

RIGHT: The raven is common in Alaska Native folklore, and in myth and legend around the world.

BELOW: Arctic ground squirrel, Brooks Range. Ground squirrels nearly double their weight in the summer in preparation for winter hibernation.

A Dall ewe and lamb easily negotiate the snowy slopes of the Arctic National Wildlife Refuge. When pursued by predators, Dall sheep retreat to the rocky crags for safety.

Two mew gull chicks attempt to elude mosquitoes and predators on a chunk of ice near Bear Glacier. Mew gulls nest on cliff ledges, sea stacks, and inaccessible locations on the mainland.

RIGHT: The conspicuous prints of a brown bear on a beach in Katmai National Park.

FACING PAGE: Two brown bears wrestle on the tidal flats. A bear will shake its head left and right to indicate to another bear it would like to play, then wait for the same as a response.

This bull moose's rack is more than 70 inches wide; the blood on its antlers indicates that it has just shed its velvet.

LEFT: A young grizzly bear in Denali National Park seems to consider this tree its adversary, snapping branches and biting limbs.

BELOW: Too tired to take flight after a scuffle with another owl, this short-eared owl gazes at the photographer for a portrait.

ABOVE: A wolverine in the Central Alaskan Brooks Range protects its find: a piece of caribou hide frozen in the ice. Wolverines are scavengers and will travel up to 40 miles per day in search of food.

RIGHT: Arctic foxes often follow polar bears onto the pack ice in search of food. As omnivores, arctic foxes survive on anything from scavenged carcasses to small mammals, seabirds, eggs, and berries.

RIGHT: A lesser scaup prepares for take-off, Tetlin Wildlife Refuge. The birds feed on aquatic plants and crustaceans.

BELOW: Three stilt sandpipers sleep while they wait for the sun to rise and melt the ice separating them from their food, Central Arctic Coastal Plain.

White-sided dolphins surface and dive for onlookers in Resurrection Bay. While primarily a deepwater species, they are being spotted more frequently in inland waters and seem to enjoy bow riding, surfing, and somersaulting.

ABOVE: A Steller's jay alights on an outcropping near Miller's Landing.

LEFT: With a mixture of curiosity and fear, two brown bears stick close to their mother as they watch adult bears fight over fishing turf, coast of Katmai National Park.

LEFT: Brown bear triplets stand up for a better view of their mother catching salmon, Katmai National Park. Litter size ranges from one to four cubs, two being the most common.

FAR LEFT: Mountain goats graze as snow gives way to the verdant vegetation of spring, near Exit Glacier in Kenai Fjords National Park.

FACING PAGE: This musk ox cow keeps a close eye on its playful newborn calf. Calves are born in the spring to cows two years and older.

BELOW: A horned puffin sits on a cliff near its nesting hole on Resurrection Bay. Puffins spend the winter in large groups on the open sea.

A bull caribou grazes on
vegetation while Denali
peaks through the clouds.
This bull is within a day
of losing its velvet.

A black bear and two cubs roam the area near Exit Glacier. Cubs remain
with their mothers through the first winter following their birth.

Snowshoe hare in the Arctic
National Wildlife Refuge.
The hind feet of these hares
are large and covered with
dense fur, adapting them for
travel in the deep snow.

A moose calf licks its lips as it wakes from a nap, Kenai Peninsula. Calves stay with their mothers until approximately one year of age.

This female white-tailed ptarmigan attempts to lead the photographer away from where it has nested. This hen calls the area near Exit Glacier, Kenai Fjords National Park, home.

FACING PAGE: This brown bear cub tries to wrestle a fish from its mother on the coast of Katmai National Park. Cubs typically separate from their mothers at age two.

LEFT: A trumpeter swan takes to the air. Trumpeters are the largest species of waterfowl in the world.

BELOW: A downy Pacific loon chick swims in a small pond on the Central Arctic Coastal Plain. Loons mate for life and return to the same breeding areas year after year.

LEFT: Two precocious mountain goat kids, near Exit Glacier. Nannies and kids gather to form nursery flocks.

FAR LEFT: Black-legged kittiwakes nest on steep cliffs to evade predators, Resurrection Bay.

This polar bear family is watchful of an approaching bear. Cubs remain with their mothers until three years of age; in the wild, polar bears can live up to 25 years.

Male silver or Coho salmon negotiating shallow water in spawning stream.

PHOTO BY TOM & PAT LEESON

Bull walrus in fog created by the heat-generating congregation of walruses and the cool coastal air.
PHOTO BY TOM & PAT LEESON

RIGHT: Bald eagles seek perches after an early spring snowstorm, Homer Sand Spit, south-central Alaska. In fall, around Haines, up to 3,000 bald eagles gather for the salmon run.

BELOW: An arctic fox, perfectly camouflaged, searches for food on the North Slope.

LEFT: A porcupine hides in the brush, Brooks Range. Porcupines do not hibernate but instead stay active in the winter months, feeding at night and during warm weather.

BELOW: A mink searches the low tide line for a meal, Prince William Sound. Minks eat a wide variety of foods including fish, birds, eggs, crabs, clams, insects, and small mammals.

This bull moose is shedding its velvet, late summer, Denali National Park. Once the rut begins, bulls will try to gather cows together, becoming much more aggressive.

FACING PAGE: This sow grizzly, with triplets, has been fitted with a radio collar. Biologists are monitoring its movements near the oil town of Prudhoe Bay.

BELOW: A beaver swims across one of many small lakes and ponds in the state. Beavers store food for winter in underground caches.

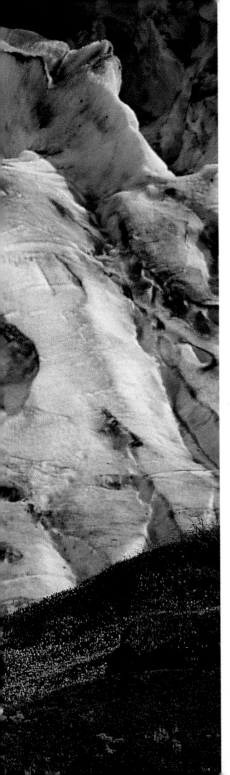

FAR LEFT: Black bear sow and cub wander where the tundra meets Exit Glacier.

LEFT: Tens of thousands of birds, including this tufted puffin, can be found nesting on the steep cliffs of Chiswell Marine Sanctuary. Puffins are awkward in flight but are skillful swimmers.

BELOW: Yellow-billed loon on a pond in the Brooks Range. This is the largest species of loon.

ABOVE: The grand silhouette of a bald eagle at sunset, Homer Sand Spit, south-central Alaska.

LEFT: Caribou and newborn calves move north through the Coastal Plain of the Arctic National Wildlife Refuge. The cows come to the area for the nutrient-rich Alaska cotton sprouts, which help them create a more nutritious milk for their young.

PHOTO BY TONY FISCHBACH

The son of an ice-cream store owner and a school teacher, Steven Kazlowski grew up in Valley Stream, New York, just outside of Queens. Steven earned a degree in marine biology from Towson State University, in Baltimore. After working briefly in his field, he set out for Alaska to become a wildlife photographer. Initially working part-time on fishing boats and in construction jobs to support his dream, Steven now works full-time as an independent photographer. His photos have been featured recently in *Audubon, Backpacking,* and *Canadian National Geographic* magazines. He also produces and distributes his own line of postcards and other print products. He spends most of the year exploring Alaska.

www.lefteyepro.com/